NOW WE ARE SIXTY

NOW WE ARE SIXTY
BY CHRISTOPHER MATTHEW
DECORATIONS BY DAVID ECCLES

VIKING

For
Bertie Lomas

VIKING
Published by the Penguin Group
Penguin Putnam Inc., 375 Hudson Street,
New York, New York 10014, U.S.A.
Penguin Books Ltd, 27 Wrights Lane,
London W8 5TZ, England
Penguin Books Australia Ltd, Ringwood,
Victoria, Australia
Penguin Books Canada Ltd, 10 Alcorn Avenue,
Toronto, Ontario, Canada M4V 3B2
Penguin Books (N.Z.) Ltd, 182–190 Wairau Road,
Auckland 10, New Zealand

Penguin Books Ltd, Registered Offices:
Harmondsworth, Middlesex, England

First American edition
Published in 2001 by Viking Penguin,
a member of Penguin Putnam Inc.

1 3 5 7 9 10 8 6 4 2

Illustrations by David Eccles (with sincere and affectionate
tribute to the genius of Ernest Shepard)

LIBRARY OF CONGRESS CATALOGING IN PUBLICATION DATA
Matthew, Christopher, 1939–
Now we are sixty / by Christoper Matthew ; decorations by
David Eccles.
p.   cm.
ISBN 0-670-03047-3
1. Aging—Poetry. 2. Humorous poetry, English.
I. Title:Now we are 60. II. Title.
PR6063.A862 N69 2001
821'.914—dc21   2001026323

This book is printed on acid-free paper. ∞

Printed in the United States of America
Set in Goudy Old Style MT

INTRODUCTION

The film actor Tony Curtis was once asked by the host of an American TV chat show how he would sum up his life. 'When I was a very young man,' Curtis said, 'I arrived in Hollywood without any money, checked into a cheap motel, showered, shaved and then I came here to talk to you.'

Having recently turned sixty, I know just how he feels. One minute I was looking at my parents and their friends and wondering what it would be like to be as old as them; the next thing I knew, I was. Mind you, in their day sixty-year-olds *were* old. Elderly, certainly, and resigned to a slow, slippered twilight. I, on the other hand, am nothing if not a product of my age, and thus do not feel a second older than I did ten years ago—or even twenty.

Who am I kidding, though? Another ten years and my Biblical quota will be up. Like it or not I have joined the ranks of the zimmer brigade. This collection is by way of marking, if not celebrating, my new-found status.

I could have waited for a year or two to ensure a first-hand account of the pleasures and pains of being an oldie, but decided I'd better crack on while the going is good and before someone asks me to show my bus pass.

How best, though, to run the unfamiliar gamut of geriatricity? A *vade mecum* for the elderly, however liberally laced with jokes, could all too easily decline into a catalogue of whinge and woe. Pith, wit and pleasure are more the order of the day— tempered with the merest touch of melancholia.

And then it suddenly occurred to me. Here I am, even more baffled by life than when I was a small boy. I had already purloined A.A. Milne's title and twisted it to my purpose, so why not pick the best of the poems he wrote for six-year-olds and re-write them for sixty-year-olds?

So I have.

CONTENTS

CLUBMAN
(*after* SOLITUDE)

I have this club where I go
    When I'm feeling unwanted,
I have this club in Soho
    Where I can be me;
I have this club—whacko!—
Where no one ever says 'No';
They all know what I'm there for—and
    Just look after me.

LET'S ALL GO MAD
(*after* BUCKINGHAM PALACE)

'They're changing sex at Buckingham Palace!'
Murgatroyd mutters with undisguised malice.
'Roger is marrying one of the guard—
Bugger whose bearskin reeks of pomade,
                              Called Alice.'

'They're a goal or two short of a chukka at
   Highgrove!'
Gutteridge growls and gesticulates. 'By Jove!
There's luvvies and duvvies and comics galore;
They say Stephen Fry had to sleep on the floor
                              In an alcove.'

'They've all gone bonkers down at the Bailey,'
Skeffington shrieks like a capercaillie.
'One of the judges—you'll never guess who—
Summed up in the nude and crooned to a u-
                              kelele.'

'They're losing their grip at New Labour Towers,'
Butterworth bellows and groans and glowers.
'They used to have *men* in the Cabinet Room;
Now it's woofters and poofters and goodness
   knows whom.
                           All showers!'

'They're out of their trees in the Lord's Pavilion,'
Somerville splutters, his face vermilion.
The Long Room has been irrevocably lost;
It's a loo now, for ladies, and what's more, it cost
                             A million.'

'They're going bananas round at the Garrick,'
Henderson hollas in tones tartaric.
'Milne left a fortune, to everyone's glee,
But they still charge a fortune for afternoon tea.
                             Barbaric!'

CUTTING EDGE
(*after* HAPPINESS)

Tom had a
Brand New
Personal Computer;
Tom was
Plugged
On the
Internet;
Tom had
The Works,
But was
Techno-illiterate,
And that
Was pretty
   Much
   That.

INSOMNIA
(*after* IN THE DARK)

I've been to dinner,
　And over-eaten,
　　And drunk a brandy or three;
I've taken a couple
　Of Alka-Seltzer,
　　And had a jolly good pee;
I've settled the cat,
　And I've locked the back door,
　　And I've turned on the burglar alarm,
And I've laid up for breakfast,
　And kissed the wife,
　　Which never does one any harm.

So—here I am in the dark awake,
　The clock has just struck two;

I've counted sheep
And bonked Bo-Peep,
And still I'm nowhere nearer sleep;
Here I am in the dark awake,
What *am* I going to do?
I can't turn the light on and watch the telly,
I can't read a book or quote bits of Shelley,
I can't nip downstairs and eat tagliatelle,
It'd only wake up the old moo.

I'm kissing Nicole Kidman . . .
I'm winning the Nobel . . .

I think I must be dying—
   I'm well.
I'm halfway up Mount Everest . . .
   I'm milking a prize cow . . .
I'm a two-time Oscar winner . . .
   I'm a WOW.
I've won a boardroom battle . . .
   I'm feeling really chuffed . . .
I'll be all right tomorrow . . .

   . . . . . .
I'll win the fight tomorrow . . .

   . . . . . .
I'll see . . .
      the light . . .
         tomorrow . . .
       (*Heigh-ho!*)
            I'm stuffed.

SIR JOHN'S FANCY
(*after* KING JOHN'S CHRISTMAS)

Sir John was quite a vain man—
  He liked his share of praise.
When people didn't speak to him,
  He'd sulk for days and days.
And when he put his gear on
  And jogged around the park,
He wouldn't go when it was light,
He said he thought it wasn't right,
His Lycra shorts were much too tight—
  He went when it was dark.

Sir John was quite a vain man—
  He fussed about his weight.
He wished that it would disappear
  So he could have a date.
And every day he weighed himself
  And crossed his fingers hard,
And groaned and grumbled loud and long,
And said, 'This damned machine's gone wrong.
I'm not surprised, it's from Hong Kong,'
  And threw it in the yard.

Sir John was quite a vain man—
　　He wasn't one to search
For deeper, hidden meanings,
　　And never went to church.
He didn't hold with vicars—
　　'Cut out the middle man
And deal direct,' was what he preached.
But when he saw the size he'd reached
And felt just like a whale that's beached,
　　He tried a different plan.

So, every night at midnight,
　　And sometimes after that,
He'd make himself a cup of tea
　　And then put out the cat,
And slip into his jim-jams
　　And brush his thinning hair
And bend his knee beside the bed
And clasp his hands and bow his head
(As all men do who are well-bred)
　　And offer up this prayer:

'Dear Lord, I'm not a bad sort,
  Like some that you must know,
Who fiddle their expenses
  And don't pay what they owe.
I'm not what you'd call greedy,
  I never stuff my face;
Yet, Lord, however hard I try
To cut out puds and self-deny,
Still fatter grow my hip and thigh.
  Look kindly on my case.'

'I have this secretary—
  I call her Freckly Jane.
She's not what you'd call pretty,
  And she's not what you'd call plain.
I have no base intentions,
  I'd like to be her chum
And sometimes ask her out to lunch;
But when it comes, Lord, to the crunch,
She looks away. I have a hunch
  She's laughing at my tum.'

'Forget about our share price
    And forget about my rise,
And all the firm's elaborate plans
    To Europeanize.
I don't need money
    And I don't want fame;
I've got my knighthood,
    I've made my name.
But oh, Lord of Mercy, pardon my distaste,
    And grant me a nice trim thirty-four inch waist!'

Sir John went to the office
    And smiled at Freckly Jane,
And, to his great amazement,
    She smiled right back again.
He said, 'I'm no Adonis . . . '
    She said, 'I'm no Monroe.
You may not be a superstar—
I like you just the way you are;
You're rather like my late papa—
    A cuddly Romeo.'

THE MORAL OF THIS STORY
SHOULD MAKE US ALL FEEL WARM:
GOD MOVES IN A
MYSTERIOUS WAY
HIS WONDERS
TO PERFORM!

LOST DREAMS
(*after* CHERRY STONES)

Golfer, Actor,

Chiropractor,

Property Developer,

Novelist,
Priest—

And what about a Banker,
Publisher, Painter,
Animal Behaviourist,
Or Drag Artiste?
What about a Bookie—or a Chef on the Telly?
What about a Tour Guide who's an expert on New
    Delhi?
And the man who asks a fortune for financial
    advice?
Or the smoothie picture dealer who sells dodgy
    merchandise?
What about a journalist who dreams up silly
    stories?
Or a little man from Yorkshire who reinvents the
    Tories?

Oh, there's such a lot of things I wish I'd had the
   time to do—
With as little hope of doing them as fly to Timbuktu!

ENCOUNTERS
(*after* PUPPY AND I)

I met a Girl in the National Gallery;
We got chatting,
Girl and I.
'What do you think of this bloke, da Vinci?'
   (I said to the Girl). 'I don't know why
But you remind me of La Gioconda.'
   She said, 'Sorry, I really must fly.'

I met a Dog in Kensington Gardens—
Nice dog, long tail,
One black eye.
'Fancy a walk to the Round Pond and back?'
  (I said to the Dog and slapped my thigh).
He gave me a look that said, 'You're joking!'
  Cocked his leg and walked on by.

I met a Man on Clapham Common;
We got chatting,
Man and I.
'What are you up to at two in the morning?'
  (I said to the Man—I can't think why).
'Fancy a drink and a bite in Brixton?'
  He suddenly said. I thought, 'Aye, aye!'

I met a Woman in Marks and Spencer—
Raincoat, head scarf,
Trolley piled high.
'Fancy a hand with that lot, darling?'
   (I said to the Woman and winked my eye).
'The car's outside, you're no Will Carling,
   But you *are* my husband. Oh well—nice try.'

SUNSHINE
(*after* TWINKLETOES)

When the sun
Twinkles on the bonnet of my Golf GT,
When the sky
Is as gloriously blue as blue can be,
Then, heigh-ho,
Off I go.
The air's as fresh as grass,
On the Newbury by-pass—
Hallo . . . Oh no!
I'm in a bloody traffic jam!

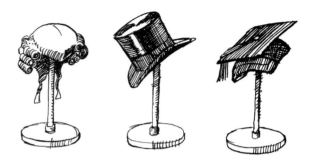

BRIEF LIVES
(*after* THE FOUR FRIENDS)

Nick is a barrister—a very well-heeled one,
   Hugh is an actor on a very fast track,
James is a surgeon with rooms in Harley Street,
     And Jeff is an out-of-work hack.

Hugh was a dandy in an Eton collar,
   James was at Westminster and flew sky-high,
Nick was a Wykehamist and classical scholar,
     And Jeff was at Liverpool High.

James had rooms by the river in Magdalen,
    Nick played cricket and rowed for The House,
Hugh got ahead by merely dawdlin',
        And Jeff was a hard-working scouse.

James had a maisonette in Little Venice,
    Nick took the room at the end of the hall,
Hugh shared a bed with a boy called Dennis,
        And Jeff cooked and cleaned for them all.

Hugh got an agent and lived on promises,
    Nick ate dinners in Lincoln's Inn,
James bought a skeleton and studied at Thomas's,
        And Jeff joined a rag in King's Lynn.

James marched about with a ruddy great stethoscope,
  Nick passed his finals and went to the Bar,
Hugh got a break and a part in a telly soap,
        And Jeff wrote for *Which Abattoir?*

Hugh got the lead in the new Robert Redford,
  James made his name in the transplant field,
Nick won a famous murder case in Bedford,
        And Jeff got the boot and appealed.

James has a place in Mustique where he winters,
  Hugh went to Hollywood and never came back,
Nick got a peerage and dines with the Pinters,
        And Jeff's still an out-of-work hack.

LONDON STREETS
(*after* LINES AND SQUARES)

Whenever I walk down a London street,
I take great care where I put my feet.
   And I watch for the gobs
   And the doggies' big jobs
That lie there in piles, some sloppy, some neat,
Waiting for people to squidge with their feet.
   And I tiptoe around
   With my eyes on the ground
And wonder what horror I'm next going to meet.

And the harder I look, I give you my word,
The more I seem drawn to the tiniest turd.
And the dogs see me coming and say, 'Here's a sap.
Let's nip round the corner and have a good crap.
He's wearing those shoes that have crinkly soles,
With lots of small ridges and dozens of holes.
And if we distract him by having a piddle,
Nine times out of ten he'll tread slap in the middle.'
There's nothing more pleases a dog's simple wit
Than to hear the familiar cry of 'Oh, shit!'

SALOON BAR ROMEOS
(*after* THE LITTLE BLACK HEN)

Hebblethwaite and Hopwood,
　Fothergill and Fenn
And Bob Stanford-Dingley
　Are five grown men . . .
And all of them are ogling
　Our barmaid, Jen.

She's just thirty,
    They're twice that;
Hopwood's a tax man,
    Fothergill's a prat.
Hebblethwaite's retired
    After years in the bank.
Fenn calls her 'darling';
    She looks blank.

Hopwood whistles,
    Fenn looks lame;
Jen says, 'Now then,
    What's your game?'
'What game's that, then?'
    Dingley leers.
The others all snigger,
    One of them cheers.

Jen says, 'Okay—
   I may look dumb.
I don't have a boyfriend,
   I live with my mum.
I'm not very rich
   And I'm no Kate Moss,
But any more nonsense,
   I'm calling my boss.'

     Hebblethwaite and Hopwood,
        Fothergill and Fenn
      And Bob Stanford-Dingley
         Are five old men.
      They've given up ogling
        And chatting up Jen.
For dear little Jen is *much* too wary,
  Sweet little Jen is FAR too chary,
Nothing about her is airy-fairy—
  She could eat them all for tea!

MEETING
(*after* MARKET SQUARE)

I had a meeting,
A big client meeting,
In Stockport in Cheshire
   Which was rather a pain.
So I rang through to Susie,
My PA from Fulham,
And asked her to book me
   On the eight o'clock train.

Then I ordered a taxi—a minicab from Wimbledon
(Clapped-out Merc with a left-hand drive).
'I've got to go to Euston, I've got to get there early
   To pick up my ticket,' I tried to explain.

I went to a party,
A big drinks party,
A farewell piss-up
    For a friend called Ken.
I didn't really want to,
I said I'd be home early.
'Oh, don't be such a pooper.'
    'Just a quick one, then.'

I picked up the phone and I rang my number.
('Please leave a message after the bleep.')
'It's only me, darling, I'm still in a meeting.
    I'll catch the eight-thirty, I'll be home by ten.'

I had a whisky,
I had another whisky,
And then I had a third
    And another one, too.
I started with a Perrier,
And all the best intentions,
But then I thought 'Oh, bugger it!'
    And met my Waterloo.

So I missed the eight-thirty, and the nine, and the
        next one.
I nearly caught the ten o'clock, but missed that, too.
So then I caught a stopping train—not the one to
        Wimbledon—
    And ended up in Basingstoke, and got in at two.

    I had a headache,
    A bloody great headache,
    I stood on the doorstep
        And didn't feel well.
    I looked and I waited,
    A dozen Mercs passed me,
    But none was a minicab,
        As far as I could tell.

So I walked to the road where they always have
        black cabs.
('Push comes to shove, mate, you can't beat a black
        cab.')
And I stood on the pavement outside the Tandoori,
    But could I find a free cab? Could I, bloody hell?

I had a brainwave,
A brilliant brainwave,
I got out my mobile
    And telephoned the wife.
The au pair answered—
Nice girl, big boobs,
Can't speak English
    To save her life.

So I tried a spot of French and a smidgen of Italian.
('Est-ce que la signora est dans la casa?')
But she thought I was a salesman, or a pervert, or a
        plumber,
    So she gasped and she giggled and she shrieked
      for dear life.

MIGRAINE

I had a migraine,
A bloody great migraine;
I took my migraine
   To the Northern Line.
But they'd closed the station—
'Incident at Stockwell;
There won't be any service
   Till half past nine.'

So I went round the corner and stood at the bus stop.
(Me and the world and his wife at the bus stop.)
'I want to get to Euston,' I said to the inspector.
   'You and fifty others, mate. Back of the line.'

I've got a meeting,
A sort of a meeting,
More an appointment
    At You-Know-Where.
I go every Thursday
And stand in the dole queue
And sign on the dotted,
    Like everyone there.

So I'm sorry for the ones who got to the meeting,
I'm sorry for the au pair who's back in Bologna,
I'm sorry for the wife who's gone to her mother's,
    'Cos I'm sorry for 'most everyone, 'most
        everywhere!

BROKEN-DOWN LILY
(*after* DAFFODOWNDILLY)

She wore a grotty blanket,
　　She wore a woolly hat,
She pushed a Sainsbury's trolley,
　　Piled high with this and that.
She sat in Piccadilly
　　With a dog with dreadful mange
And said to all who passed her,
　　'Got any spare change?'

MARRIAGE
(*after* A THOUGHT)

If I were Bess and Bess were Me,
Then she'd sit here and I'd make tea.
If Bess were Me and I were Bess,
I wouldn't ever wear this dress.

MOBILE MAN
(*after* DOWN BY THE POND)

I'm on the train.
Don't pull silly faces; don't you moan;
Can't you see that I'm on the phone?
'Hallo, love! It's me! Everything okay?
We're stuck here in Doncaster. We'll soon be on our way.
    We're due out at seven—
    Should be with you at eleven.
        I'll keep you posted—
            From the train.'

Hi! I'm in the theatre!
Don't tut like that, you stupid old crone!
Can't you see that I'm on the phone?
'What was that, Charlie? I got your fax.
That ballpark figure, was that *plus* tax?
  I'll call you back tomorrow.
  No—tomorrow! TOMORROW!
    Can't talk now, I'M IN
      THE THEATRE!'

MOTHER
(*after* DISOBEDIENCE)

Tom, Clare,
Crispin and Clementine,
Oliver, Jane and me
Gave much
Thought to old Mother
When she was ninety-three.
Tom, Clare,
Crispin and Clementine,
Oliver, Jane and their three
Did plenty of talking and fussing and squawking, but
  left all the doing to me.

One day
Our dear old Mother
Dressed in her Sunday best,
Left a note
In the kitchen:

'I don't want to be a pest.
I've just popped out
To New Zealand,
I've gone on a bit of a spree,
I'll visit my brother, his wife and my mother, and
    be back in time for tea.'

The police
Alerted all mobiles:
'Elderly woman in grey—
Answers to Mrs Macdougall,
Could be heading your way.
Thinks she's
Off to New Zealand,
Handle with extra care.
She could be doolally, so be nice and pally—and
    try not to give her a scare.'

Tom, Clare,
Crispin and Clementine
(Known to her friends as Clem),
Got straight
On to the blower,
Said that one couldn't blame *them*.
Clementine
Said, 'Well I never!
Frankly,' she said, 'if she
Can't be left on her own, she should be in a home—
somewhere nice down in Kent by the sea.'

Poor dear
Silly old Mother
Was found feeding ducks in the park,
With a tramp
With a trolley from Tesco,
Piled like a nomadic camp.
She said,
'Lovely to see you—
This is my young brother, Roy.
He's such a nice chap, and he's not changed a scrap
since he was a dear little boy.'

(*To be spoken, very solemnly and clearly—as though to a backward child*)

  'T, C,
  C, C,
  O, J and me
  Can't look
  After you, M*****,
  Now you're 93.'
  'Stuff and
  Nonsense,' said M*****.
  'If I can cross the sea,
And visit my brother, his wife and my mother,
 there's nothing much wrong with ME!'

AUTUMN AFTERNOON
(*after* SPRING MORNING)

Where are we going? I wish I knew.
To Bali? Or Mali? Or even Peru?
On a luxury cruise with our friends John and Prue?
Somewhere, anywhere. Haven't a clue.

Where are we going? The years drift by.
Last year we went for a week to Dubai.
I tried to play golf; I thought I would fry.
It was so bloody boring, I wanted to cry.

If I were a sailor, I'd pop down to Cowes,
Or drift down the Nile on a couple of dhows.
If I were a skier, I'd book up a chalet,
In Wengen or Mürren or down in the Valais.

Where *are* we going? The brochure's a-glow
With sunshine and beaches and tours of Bordeaux,
And silver-haired couples in evening dress
Enjoying the pleasures of bouillabaisse.

We've been on safari, we've been to Hong Kong,
We've been to Bangkok, in a boat, up a klong.
We've been to Vienna and heard the Boys' Choir,
And sat eating clams on Cape Cod round a fire.

Is there anywhere left, now the world is so small,
That hasn't been ruined by touristic sprawl?
Perhaps we should sit here and watch the night fall,
And get ready to make the last journey of all.

INFLATION
(*after* WIND ON THE HILL)

No one can fathom,
Nobody knows,
It's simply a mystery
Where money goes.

I went to the cash-point
   This morning at ten,
Took out fifty quid and
   Went back home again.

I popped into Tesco's,
   Bought fish for the cat,
And filled half a basket
   With this and with that.

I bought a few flowers
   To brighten the house;
Just a couple of bunches
   And one for the spouse.

I paid off the daily,
   Gave ten to the kids,
And, wouldn't you know it,
   I'm back on the skids.

THE THREE TOE-RAGS
(*after* THE THREE FOXES)

Once upon a time there were three little toe-rags,
Who didn't have jobs, and they lived in flea-bags.
They all had vodaphones to call their mates up,
And they travelled on tube trains and nicked flash
handbags.

They hated all blacks and they hated all Saudis,
They went to the footie and they fought with rowdies.
They broke into garages in quiet little mewses,
And they went joy-riding in nice new Audis.

They drank tinned lager and they sniffed at glue tins,
They smashed shop window-fronts with upturned
    dustbins.
But they soon grew tired of these harmless pastimes,
So they stole some handguns and did small bust-ins.

That's all that I know of the three little toe-rags,
Who travelled on tube trains and nicked flash
    handbags,
And didn't have jobs and lived in flea-bags,
And broke into premises brandishing handguns—
Except that any could be one of my grandsons.

RUDE HEALTH
(*after* POLITENESS)

When people enquire
After me health-wise,
'Not bad, considering,' I usually say.
When my friends ask me
How I am feeling,
I tend to tell them, 'I'm better today.'
I always answer,
I always tell them,
If they seem really
Interested . . .

BUT MORE OFTEN THAN NOT

I wish

They'd bugger off and mind their own business.

STREET THEATRE
(*after* JONATHAN JO)

Wherever I go
My mouth's like an 'O'
Because life is so full of surprises.
When I walk down the street
I am certain to meet
Performers in various guises.

If I fancy a row
   With an ugly low-brow,
I'm bound to get into a brawl
   With a bloke whose best trick
   Is being violently sick
And then peeing over a wall.

Or a kid on his skates
Who exterminates
All and sundry whose path he may cross;
And when I point out
He's being a lout,
Shouts, 'Sod off, mate. I don't give a toss.'

IN THE LOO
(*after* AT THE ZOO)

There are piddles and puddles and oodles
   of fag ends and tissues and stuff,
There are strips of soggy old cardboard,
   and a pong that is seriously rough.
There are doors without any handles,
   and holders without paper, too,
But I just stare at the ceiling, when I go into the loo.

There are driers with swivelling nozzles,
   and toilets with dirty brown rings,
There are rusty machines full of pictures
   of nobbly, bobbly things.
And holes where there used to be packets,
   and a broken window or two,
But I just stare at the ceiling, when I go into the loo.

There are cubicles riddled with scribbles,
   and strange anatomical shapes,
And pedestals gushing like rivers
   over objects like large yellow grapes.
And a room for the superintendent,
   who never says 'How do you do?'
But I just stare at the ceiling, when I go into the loo.

RADIO FOUR
(*after* RICE PUDDING)

What is the matter with Radio Four?
I can't find a programme to save my life,
And nor can my barber or dentist or wife.
What *is* the matter with Radio Four?

Whatever has happened to On Your Farm,
With those wonderful breakfasts of bangers and beer,
And porridge and fish cakes and eggs and good cheer,
And stories and insights and humour and charm?

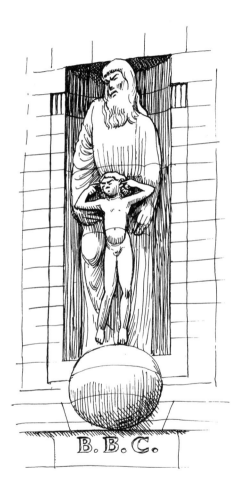

59

Oh, why have they shuffled those favourites of yore?
It can't be good sense, it must be a hunch
To move lunchtime Archers to just *after* lunch.
Oh, *isn't* the latest Controller a bore?

And who are these people whose views they all
    sought?
Who swore we all needed *three hours* of Today
But ten minutes *less* of the news at midday,
And nothing to speak of of sport?

What *is* the matter with Radio Four?
I'm not an old fart and I'm not an old bore
Or a grumpy old bugger like Evelyn Waugh,
But it doesn't half stick in my craw!

AWOL
(*after* MISSING)

Has anybody seen my wife?

I left the house for half a minute.
When I went out, she was certainly in it.
I walked to the shop at the top of the road,
And when I say 'walked', I really mean 'strode'.
I was back in a tick—you could hardly say 'knife'.
Has *anyone* seen my wife?

Maria, have you seen my wife?

My wife? You remember? The
    mother of Tim?
The boy you look after? D'you
    remember him?
No, I haven't lost *Tim*; it's his
    mother I'm after.
Now what's so funny? It's no
    cause for laughter.

It's early days yet. She'll be back soon.
She walked out like this in the middle of June.
She didn't go far—
And she left the car.

Has *anybody* seen my wife?

THE QUEEN'S PICKLE
(*after* THE KING'S BREAKFAST)

The Duke asked
The Queen, and
The Queen asked
The Chancellor:
'Could one have some extra
For the Royal Board and Bed?'
The Queen rang
The Chancellor,
The Chancellor
Said, 'Prudence, Ma'am,
I'll go and ask
The Think
Tank
Before they all see red.'

The Chancellor
Thought, 'Sod it,'
And rang the boys
At Demos.
'Any chance of extra
For the Royal Board and Bed?'

The Demos boys
Said, 'Joking!
You can go and tell
Her Majesty
The thinking now is favouring
A President instead.'

The Chancellor
Said, 'Thrifty!'
And went to
Her Majesty.
He winked with his good eye and
Said, 'I'm not well bred.
Pardon me not bowing,
But the *on dit* in the country
Is that private life is pleasant if
It's comfortably
Led.'

The Queen
Said, 'Eeeow,'
And went to
See Edinburgh.
'You mentioned some extra for
The Royal Board and Bed.
According to
Young Gordon,
Retiring
Is an option.
Would one care to try some
Retirement
Instead?'

The Duke said,
'Bollocks!'
And then he said,
'Oh bugger it!'
The Duke yelled, 'Bastards!'
And went brick red.
'Nobody,'
He barked,
'Could call me
Difficult,
But frankly,
Put it this way,
I'd be better
Orf dead.'

The Queen snapped,
'Philip!'
And carpeted
The Chancellor.
The Chancellor
Said, 'Now, now,
Careful how you tread.
We in
New Labour
Are hardly
Pro-Monarchy.
Push your luck, you'll end up
In a council house instead.'

The Queen said,
'Cobblers!'
And called up
Her bankers.
The Manager said,
'Money, ma'am?
You're hardly in the red.'
'Good,' said the Queen
As she tripped on a corgi.
'Great,' said the Duke
As he kissed his wife
Tenderly.
'Stuff 'em,' they said
As they drove down to Windsor.
'When one's as
Rich as we are,
One's one's own Way Ahead!'

YAKKITY
(*after* HOPPITY)

Anthea Musk-Rat goes
Yakkity, yakkity,

Yakkity, yakkity, yak.
I casually mention
I've got hypertension—
I might as well talk to a sack.

If she stopped gabbing she'd die of inertia,
Put on the veil
And hop off to Persia.
That's why she always goes
Yakkity, yakkity,
Yakkity,
Yakkity,
Yak.

WRINKLIES
(*after* THE MORNING WALK)

When Viv and I go to the shops
For milk and bread and cheese and chops,
We look at all the wrinklies there,
Who shuffle round the shelves and stare,

And tell ourselves when we are old
Our hands won't shake, we won't lose hold.
And when we're halfway home, we find
We've left the cheese and chops behind.

ETERNAL YOUTH
(*after* THE DOORMOUSE AND THE DOCTOR)

There once was a health freak who, morning and
    night,
Ate chlorella (dark green) and magnesium (white).
He was fit as a flea and thin as a bean
On magnesium (white) and chlorella (dark green).

He never ate meat and he never touched fish,
He was strict vegetarian, dish upon dish.
And he ran through the park with his head in a
    snood,
And did yoga each night on the floor in the nude.

In winter he wore open sandals with thongs
And did deep meditation with incense and gongs.
And however he felt, whether cool or uptight,
He ate chlorella (green) and magnesium (white).

He thought cars and buses polluted the air,
So he rode an old bike or he walked everywhere.
He worked twice a week for the Friends of the Earth,
And several similar causes of worth.

He'd never been married and lived with his mum;
When she died, in her nineties, he lodged with a chum
Who managed a health-shop in deepest East Sheen
And kept him supplied with chlorella (dark green).

A colleague (not bearded) said, 'Am I a bore
If I ask you what all of these tablets are for?
I know one is algae that floats in the sea,
Or is that the stuff that you get from a bee?'

The health nutter chuckled and uttered *bons mots*,
About *mens* being *sana in corpus sano.*
'In a flu epidemic, I'm always all right
With chlorella (dark green) and magnesium (white).

I don't smoke, I don't drink (except for herb tea),
I'm sixty years old, but I feel twenty-three.
I could go on for ever; my future is bright,
Thanks to chlorella (green) and magnesium (white).'

'I think you mean *corpore*,' put in his friend.
'And in my opinion you're clean round the bend.
The ageing procedure you can't contravene
With a handful of pills, be they red, white or green.

Okay, so I know that it's easy to scoff,
But in my humble view you'd be far better off
With a nice bouncy girl and a week by the sea
In sunny Barbados—or even Torquay.

Take me, for example, I'm sixty next year
And I live on a diet of bangers and beer.
You can keep your brown rice and organic cuisine
And your whatsisname (white) and your thingummy
    (green).'

Old smuggy just shook his bald head and he smiled
In a way that one does with a silly young child.
But the fact is, his friend may be well overweight,
But the poor bloke himself looks a hundred and
    eight.

So, if ever you're tempted to push back the years
And to score extra points with your friends and your
    peers:
The funny thing is—anyway, in my book—
The harder you try to, the older you look.

GOLF CLUB
(*after* SHOES AND STOCKINGS)

There's a corner in the golf club where the old boys
    chat
(*Mutter, mutter, mutter . . .*
Mutter, mutter, mutter . . .)
They drink pink gin and they chew the fat
(*Mutter, mutter, mutter . . .*
Mutter, mutter, mutter . . .)
They thumb their diaries and they hum and hah,
'I can't this Friday, I'm in Leamington Spa.
How about next week? Let's try that.'
Mutter, mutter, mutter . . .
Mutter.

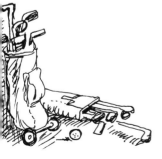

There's a room in the golf club where the trouts
    play bridge
(*Natter, natter, natter . . .*
Natter, natter, natter . . .)
There's Audrey and Rosemary and Caroline and
    Midge
(*Natter, natter, natter . . .*
Natter, natter, natter . . .)
'Two spades,' 'No trumps,' 'No bid,' 'One heart.'
They've got trapped wind and they're dying to fart,
And there's cold meat waiting at the bottom of the
    fridge.
Natter, natter, natter . .
Natter.

LIAR
(*also after* HOPPITY)

Piggy Pengelly goes
Wibbly, wobbly,
Wibbly, wobbly, wib.
If ever I hint that he
Might be a fatty,
He always resorts to a fib.

He says he'll stop snacking
    and slacking and stacking
Up mountains of blubber
And handfuls like rubber.
But *still* he goes
Wibbly, wobbly,
Wibbly,
Wobbly,
Wib.

FAITH
(*after* HALFWAY DOWN)

Just along from Harrods
Is a place
Where I sit.
There isn't any
Other place
Quite like
It.
It's not Roman Catholic,
Or quite C of E;
It's more happy-clappy
There,
Just like
Me.

The church where I go
Isn't high,
And isn't trad.
It makes me feel much better,
It makes me really glad
I'm not like other people
Who haven't found God . . .
It's difficult to
Share it with
An ordinary
Bod.

GREEK TRAGEDY
(*after* THE OLD SAILOR)

There once was a tourist who went to Corfu,
And planned so many things which he wanted to do
That as soon as he got there he went to the beach
And ate a banana, two plums and a peach.

He stared at the sky and he stared at the sea,
And he looked at the sun and he said, 'Goodness me!
If I'm not very careful I'll turn lobster pink.'
So he rubbed on some sun-block and had a good think.

And he listed the things that a chap wants to do
When he books for a fortnight in sunny Corfu.
He wanted to romp with a classical faun,
And he wanted to see where Prince Philip was born.

And he wanted to eat calamares—or squid—
And drink lots of ouzo for only a quid,
And dance on the seashore like Zorba the Greek,
And climb to a monastery high on a peak.

And he wanted to wander round Old Corfu Town,
And lie on the beach and get terribly brown,
And go on an outing to Paxos one day,
And live with some monks and be taught how to pray,

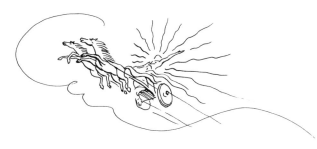

And book himself into the windsurfing school,
And visit a man with a large swimming-pool,
And water-ski madly from morning till dusk,
And buy a bouzouki and learn how to busk,

And ride on a donkey and put on a mask,
And paddle about in the water and bask,
And meet a small octopus tiddling by,
And be pulled by a speedboat and suddenly fly,

And read Gerald Durrell and Lawrence as well,
Make friends with some locals, find Prospero's Cell—
Or is that in Cyprus? He felt quite a prat.
His head started spinning: he needed a hat.

Oh, where to begin with this long list of plans?
He looked at his feet and he looked at his hands,
And he saw that they'd all turned a horrible red,
And wished he was back in his villa in bed.

And he thought of the Durrells and Old Corfu Town,
And Paxos—and Naxos—and how to go brown,
And learning to windsurf with Zorba the Faun,
And dancing about with Prince Philip at dawn . . .

And so in the end he did nothing at all;
He lay on his bed and he stared at the wall—
Recovered from sunstroke and watched his skin peel,
And thought, 'Why are holidays such an ordeal?'

GOING OUT
(*after* JOURNEY'S END)

Timothy, Timothy, where are you going,
> *Timothy, darling?*
'Just off to bomb Iraq,
Then going to look for the Ark,
Then thought I'd wrestle a Great White Shark,'
> Said Timothy.

Timothy, Timothy, what are you saying,
> *Timothy, darling?*
You know you can't fly a plane,
And it's just started to rain.
  'In that case, I'll sit down again,'
> Said Timothy.

RESIDENTS' ASSOCIATION
(*after* BAD SIR BRIAN BOTANY)

Grizelda was a battle-axe with great big bosoms;
    She wore a purple twin-set and a brooch of antique
        gold.
Gerald was her consort, a rather put-upon sort;
    They bossed the local residents, who did as they
        were told.
        'I'm Lady Rumpton (*JP*).'
            'This is Sir Gerald (*Brigadier*).'
        'He is your chairman and, I think, a fair man,
            But I wear the trousers round here.'

Grizelda had a mania for ultra-tidiness;
    The slightest hint of litter was a major cause for
        hate.
On Mondays and on Fridays and on holidays and
        High Days
    They'd march down Beechcroft Gardens in the
        most appalling bate:
        'Pick that up—*what, what!*
            Such a mess—*harrump!*'
        'It's a ruddy disgrace, just look at this place!
            It's worse than the worst refuse dump!'

Sir Gerald woke on Friday and he couldn't find the
    battle-axe;

He read his *Daily Telegraph* and sauntered to the pub;
He looked for Her Ladyship and guessed she must
    have made a slip
    And thought that it was Thursday and had gone
    off to her club.
       'Morning, *Sir* Gerald,' said the neighbour.
        'On your own, then?' he called out.
       'You may be our chairman, you may be a fair man,
        But you're nothing without the old trout.'

Sir Gerald had a gin and then he had another,
  He pulled on his old Crombie and he twiddled his
    stout stick.
He strolled back to his garden and his eyes begun to
    harden
  At the dreadful sight that greeted him and made
    him feel quite sick.
      'But we're the chairman—*but, but* . . .
        And I'm a fair man—*oh yuk!*'
      Every border and bed, every rose that he'd bred
        Was top-dressed with rubbish and muck!

Gerald and Grizelda have given up the chairmanship,
  They never use their titles; now they're 'Gerry'
    and 'poor Griz'.
They never boss a soul now, and frankly, on the
    whole now,
  They toddle round, quite mouse-like, and mind
    their own damned biz.
      'There's old Gerry.' (*Who he?*)
        'No one special' (*I see*)
      'And the scruffy old bat there? In the
          funny old hat there?'
        'She's nothing to you or to me.'

CARING SOCIETY
(*after* THE GOOD LITTLE GIRL)

Whenever I ring up, I get this reply:
  'Customer services—
  How may I help you?'
And when I have told them, they cheerfully cry:
  'Bear with me, would you?
  I'll just put you through.'

It could be the gas board, it could be BT,
It could be the council concerning our tree,
It could be the dealer about the new car,
Or a medical query that's rather bizarre—
  'Bear
  With me, I'm putting you through.'

It's always the same when they put you on hold:
   'Our lines are all busy,
   You're held in a queue.'
And, lest there be doubt, it's repeated tenfold:
   'Our lines are *still* busy,
   You're *still* in a queue.'

And so I just sit and I fume and I fret.
Is it worth hanging up? It's a pretty fair bet
That someone will answer me, just as I do.
And next time I'll go to the back of the queue
And once again hear that familiar coo:
   'Hallo . . .
   How may I help you?'

WORRIES
(*after* BUSY)

I think I've got an ulcer; I get a nasty twinge
Immediately after eating—a snack, a meal, a binge.

Perhaps I've got colitis. Or could it just be wind?
Or gastro-enteritis? Those crabmeat chunks were
   tinned.

SO
Round I go,
Unsound I go,
Snow-bound I go—
Down to the doctor's
To wait in the surgery.

And *down* I go,
To *town* I go,
And feeling like a *clown* I go:
I think I could be suffering from irritable bowel.

Or is it indigestion?
Or some form of congestion?
Or a grumbling appendix? That can really
  make you howl . . .

SO
Round I go,
Wind-bound I go,
In hope of *ultra-sound* I go;
Up-wound I go,
South-bound I go,
Right now.

Of course, I might have cancer—it could be in the
    genes.
The funny thing is yesterday I felt quite full of beans.
Perhaps it's nothing really; my tummy's just upset—
Though nowadays you never know; I wouldn't
    take a bet.

SO

Off I go,
You'll *scoff*, I know,
I've got this funny *cough*, and so,
Down to the doctor's,
To sit in the surgery.
And *pound* about,
Expound and shout,
Astound and flout
My woe.

IF
(*after* IF I WERE KING)

I often wish that I were rich,
Then life would go without a hitch.

If only I were that Bill Gates,
I'd talk with kings and be their mates.

If I were Cameron Mackintosh,
My plays would make huge piles of dosh.

Just think, if I were Melvyn Bragg,
My face would be in every mag.

If I were Mr Richard Branson,
Without the beard, I'd be quite handsome.

I bet if I were John Paul Getty,
I'd dish out money like confetti.

If I were Sultan of Brunei,
I'd sell my place and buy Versailles.

The trouble is, there's just one hitch:
I'm poor as hell, and life's a bitch.

PENSIONER
(*after* IN THE FASHION)

My banker has a pension and an index-linked one,
So does my solicitor and so does his son,
So does my accountant and so does everyone—
    They've all got pensions 'cept me.

If I saved a few bob, I would buy one;
I'd say to my broker, 'Let me try one.'
I'd ring my accountant and call out, 'Hi, hon,'
    And ask her round for tea.

Then I'd say to my banker, 'I thought I should
    mention
That, as from today, I'm a man with a pension,
And lest there should be any misapprehension,
    I'm happy as happy could be!'

CHRISTOPHER
(*after* PINKLE PURR)

Gervase was the father of Christopher—
A lively excrescence, as all concur.
His father, by contrast, was pure monochrome;
He never went out, he was always at home,
And in matters domestic he'd always defer
To his wife and the mother of Christopher.

Gervase was the father of Christopher,
A nonchalant youth who would never demur.
And the older he got, the more laid-back he grew,
While his dad fussed unduly and got in a stew.
And though he would never have uttered a slur—
'I'll *never* be like him,' said Christopher.

Gervase was the father of Christopher,
A carefree devil, as you'll infer,
And whatever the latest excitement or craze,
He never consulted pedantic Gervase.
And his father became a mere stranger, as 'twere—
'We're like chalk and blue cheese,' said Christopher.

Now Chris is the father of Peter and Paul,
And he's not like the young lad he once was at all.
He worries about quite the silliest things,
Like sunspots and robots and aeroplanes' wings.
And sometimes a terrible thought will recur:
'I'm *just* like my father,' says Christopher.

LAST CHANCE TRENDY
(*after* GROWING UP)

I wear a suit by Giorgio Armani,
I like an after-shave called Frangipani,
I've got this bird who's Azerbaijani,
    I feel like I'm twenty-three.

I've got a CD of right-on hip-hop,
I've got a Warhol print of a flip-flop,
I drive a Porsche-style Honda that's tip-top,
    Who's coming clubbing with me?

I've got a gold chain that sits in my chest-hair,
And tight-fitting trousers that flatter my derrière,
I reckon I could get off with the au pair,
    I'm just an LCT.

LIFE
(*after* THE END)

When I was One
The War had begun.

When I was Ten
It was wartime again.

When I was Twenty
I thought I knew plenty.

When I was Thirty
I liked to be flirty.

When I was Forty
I got rather sporty.

When I was Fifty
I turned very thrifty.

But now that I'm Sixty, I've got to confess
That more often than not, I couldn't care less.